UGLY CHIEF

Victoria Melody

UGLY CHIEF

OBERON BOOKS
LONDON

WWW.OBERONBOOKS.COM

First published in 2017 by Oberon Books Ltd
521 Caledonian Road, London N7 9RH
Tel: +44 (0) 20 7607 3637 / Fax: +44 (0) 20 7607 3629
e-mail: info@oberonbooks.com
www.oberonbooks.com

A catalogue record for this book is available from the British
Library.

PB ISBN: 9781786823700
E ISBN: 9781786823717

Front cover photography: Hugo Glendinning
Back cover photography: Andy Schofield

Contents

Hi Victoria,

I do hope you got home safe.

We all missed you this morning, we would have had loads of things for you to do, and we have had eleven funerals in since Friday.

Good luck with your show. If it all goes tits up, there is always a position for you here, you are a natural, and we all enjoyed your presence.

Keep in touch from all of us in Port Toilet (you are now a honorary Welsh girl) VICTORIA BLODWEN MELODY

Break a Leg Jinx

xxxxx

Gareth A. Jenkins
Funeral Director
Baglan Funeral Home

Foreword for *Ugly Chief*
Tora Colwill
Founder, The Modern Funeral and Brighton Death Forum

I run The Modern Funeral in Brighton, offering people practical and ceremonial support to create personal, meaningful funerals. We have an open and friendly approach to our undertaking, and are always looking to encourage new and honest conversations about death in the wider world. It made perfect sense then, when Vic asked to join us for a few days while she was researching *Ugly Chief*. Then and since, Vic and I have discussed the philosophies and practical realities of death and dying and I am eager to lay out some of those thoughts here.

Ugly Chief shows us the difficulties and joy a family can experience in the planning of a funeral – the pain of addressing death, and the value of discussing it and choosing how to respond to it. For me it also raises some big questions – how can our responses to death evolve – and what is it that is important about each of us that should be commemorated, and how?

Let's get a little fact out of the way – we do all die. There are no two ways around this and it seems rather silly to be entirely negative about the inevitable.

Humans respond to death in many ways throughout the world and these responses evolve over time. It is useful to recognise that what we currently understand as traditional funeral practises, are actually recent conventions. In the West especially, treatment of death as an event and an idea has changed significantly.

The dead have lately had negative representation. We honour and fetishize youth and beauty on our screens, while also filling them up with countless depictions of the dead as rotten old zombies. It's not very useful when so few of us have even seen a real dead person, and likely not to in the natural state.

We have allowed a certain professionalisation of death as well, perhaps a symbolic attempt to have control over the natural way of things. The handling of the dead is largely left to medical professionals, while their commemoration often falls within the domain of the funeral industry. This separation between us and our dead leads to a lack of understanding and of agency, and as with so much today, to the fact that checking out of this mortal coil has become a consumer act.

We actually have a lot to learn from death – it is the instigator of our creativity and a constant reminder to get perspective and make the most of things. Simplifying things can lead to more meaningful experiences.

To break it down – a funeral usually consists of practical and ceremonial elements:

> The Practical – What happens to our body when we die? – Who cares for our dead body? And how? How do we choose to dispose of what remains of our vessel?

> The Ceremonial – How do we come together to mark a death, and remember a life privately, within our communities, and culturally within our society.

Currently, here in the UK we tend to choose between burial and cremation – though the numbers of those choosing to donate their bodies to medical science, or specify that they do not want a funeral ceremony, have rocketed.

We seem to be moving away from the dramatic, theatrical burials of the Victorian era. Not least because we are running out of space for graveyards. Beautiful though they may be – graves are rented space, adorned with Victorian vanity that turn into wonky, unsafe, moss-eaten monuments to a person's life. There is not infinite space for this approach.

Natural burial offers a more sustainable, sensible burial option, and is on the rise. Established in the early 90s, there are now over 300 dedicated natural burial grounds in the UK.

They are run in a number of ways. Sometimes the graves are unmarked so the whole place becomes a monument to the person you buried there.

There may be a non-denominational chapel space there for ceremonies – or these could be simply held around the graveside.

Often people are buried in shallow three foot deep graves – this allows for aerobic decomposition and for the body to quickly be returned to nature. Most don't accept embalmed bodies as the chemicals threaten the environment.

At the moment around 70% of deaths in the UK are followed by a cremation.

Often quite church-like in appearance, it is worth reminding ourselves, that the chapel space at the crematorium is non-denominational. When using the space – you can take it over – take the crosses down if it's appropriate to do so.

The theatre of cremation is currently our most common experience of death.

Personally I found the curtain and the hydraulics confusing as a child. I knew something important was going on, but I was unsettlingly detached from it.

When you peer behind the mystery you discover that even as the curtain goes round. Your loved one might just join a queue to be cremated sometime soon. You leave them there.

These spaces are ours – you are allowed to invite yourself behind the theatre and into the operation of the place.

Around the world the ritual and practical needs of dealing with death can merge with varying degrees of impact.

Take Tibetan Sky Burial. On a mountain top where it's not possible to dig down, and with not enough trees to source wood for cremations there is a need to do something unexpected.

Bodies are laid out on the mountain top and can be cut so the meat is exposed. Vultures will fly in and carry parts of the body up into the sky – away and in different directions.

Though it may seem brutal, the function of the sky burial is simply to dispose of the remains in as generous a way as possible.

There is a certain parallel in signing up to have your organs or tissues donated, or leaving your body to medical science, or to a body farm. Putting your vessel out there to see what use it might be for others.

There are countless examples of different cultures dealing with death in interesting ways – that can seem quite alien to us – but there are inevitably things to learn from these different perspectives.

Open-air cremation could be a viable future option for us – such ceremonies are currently being facilitated in some areas of the United States.

Outdoor cremation is a familiar practice in India and there are people investigating the possibility of it becoming a real option here in the UK too – it can be a dramatic and beautiful process to watch.

The choice isn't just limited to burial vs. cremation. Different methods of body disposal are being worked on.

Around the world, there are contemporary projects being developed to offer solutions for how we might designate space for our dead in our modern cities.

The time is now for us to re-imagine a new type of death centre. A place where we could safely house our dead, honour the bodies, dispose of the vessel and commemorate each other's lives.

What solutions are there that marry the practical and the ceremonial in our modern world?

People are developing different ways of composting, and cremation by water is a relatively new alternative option – known as alkaline hydrolysis or resomation, it might be a real option here in the UK soon. Already operating in some parts of America and Canada and billed as a green alternative to cremation – it works by dissolving the body in heated alkaline water pressurized to 15 atmospheres in this tank. Body tissue is dissolved and the liquid poured into the municipal water system. The bones are then removed from the unit and processed in the same machine that is used to crush bone fragments following cremation by fire.

Though overtly clinical, this method is interesting as a green and efficient way of processing our dead.

There are no rules when it comes to funerals – just a range of expectations to manage.

As well as our own personal choices about what to do with our remains, we must also consider those who have been left behind.

As we become a more secular society we still gather, reflect and search for meaning when a death occurs. We can create beautiful spaces that can house gatherings for people of differing beliefs. Something that UGLY CHIEF can achieve as it takes over a venue.

Ugly Chief gently addresses the delicate balance between being in control of your own send-off and the funeral offering time and space for the real and emotional responses of those we leave behind.

One enormous question many people face is, what to do with the ashes? The ashes can be a highly symbolic link to the physical person who has died. Some people now opt to have ashes incorporated in tattoos or jewellery. You can have your ashes made into a firework, mixed with paint, or pressed into a vinyl record. The Undertaking project that KLF have recently embarked upon will turn your ashes into a brick that will be part of their communal people pyramid concept.

Even in this climate that is moving away from the Christian vision for a God, it still makes a lot of sense for people to get a bit spiritual when a death occurs. We must provide the space and freedom for people to express whatever that spirituality means to them.

You can hold a funeral anywhere.

I've arranged memorials in my lovely local arthouse cinema. The auditorium lends itself to gathering people together to guide them through a focused, transformative service. Photographs of the person's life on the screen are a good touch. Choosing a familiar and favourite environment can help everyone feel comfortable – while vividly remembering the person who has died.

And where could be more familiar than home? We have the freedom now to gently approach death. A DIY (Direct it Yourself) or Home Funeral means you have an intimate involvement with every stage. These tasks – the car journeys, the washing, the dressing, choosing, making, or decorating a coffin, the music and words – these are the last things you can do for somebody. They give you the opportunity to make sense of the pain and difficulty of what has happened.

We can all be more involved in the funeral process. I would have loved to have painted my granddad's coffin for example, it could have been a personal and transformative ritual...

Simple rituals can be repeated as a way of keeping us connected to our dead. Research suggests that engaging in rituals helps restore a sense of control and order at a time when we feel utterly powerless. They can help us to cope with our grief and move forward in a healthy way. The ritual act can be as simple as lighting a candle in someone's memory.

It really isn't as hard as it seems to challenge the existence of an industry between us and our dead. We can gently take more control.

The death industry does seem to be particularly slow to change. But our world, as ever, is changing. Our economy is challenged. We are filling up the finite space we have designated in our cities to house our dead.

In general, we are becoming a more secular society.

So our needs are changing – in many aspects of our lives – and these changes should be reflected in how we respond to death.

To help us negotiate all these changes, funeral directors, as gate-keepers – and the human face of the funeral industry – should guide us into achieving better experiences when we have to arrange funerals.

The role of the funeral director has evolved over time too. Conventional funeral directors adopt various roles while facilitating our funeral proceedings.

They can be Event Organisers. It's good to have somebody with a clear head to help everything go without a hitch on the day, to have a grasp on things in the confusing days leading up to the funeral. But they shouldn't steal the show – getting involved in the organisation can be really beneficial to families.

They can be Medical and Legal Officials. Many will offer embalming services, though I argue that this is an intrusive, unnecessary and expensive practice these days. However, a Funeral Director can be very useful as a liason with doctors and coroners, and as a guide through all the paperwork.

 They can be Celebrants, leading rituals and offering moral authority. A confident and experienced leader can be valuable to look to in a ceremony, but they must be flexible and attentive to the needs and styles of those attending.

And they can be Sales People. Funeral directors are running a business, and of course have financial expectations from their work. This however can lead to an urge to upsell to their clients, and to promote the ugly idea that your expenditure on a funeral is a reflection of your love. Instead, they should offer the service of streamlining people's options, of saving their clients money, and creating funerals that cost less and mean more.

Though it is difficult to take charge of these things, the benefits of the potential emotional healing can be deep and far-reaching. Taking the time to meditate on the inevitable – confronting the notion of our mortality, and the mortality of those we love – can better equip us to cope emotionally when these things do happen. Having dialogues with our nearest and dearest about these topics can have unexpected benefits.

Often taking control and personalising things does equate to saving significant sums of money on your funeral too. And let's face it – the costs are escalating – the UK national average is currently around £3700 and rising.

Thinking of ways to creatively challenge the rising costs of funerals will certainly help, and be welcomed by many.

Separating the practical and the ceremonial can be a way to keep costs down.

The possibilities are endless and the main thing is that we open up and discuss them.

With our relaxed regulations that place ownership of our dead firmly in our own hands – we are in a strong position to marry ceremony with practical considerations in a way that makes sense to us.

I like the fact that we are reminded of our connection to nature through death. The rituals surrounding this are our good habits. As we normalise the experience – giving people space for their emotions and remember to respond to death in ways that make sense to us – we broaden access to good funerals and healthy grief and bereavement processes.

I've found I've become happier through approaching death and including it in my life – it brings a kind of ultimate perspective – this is an important conversation that informs how we live. By following Vic and Mike's example we can get to work on searching out the appropriate answers together.

Working on ways to provide services and information that enable funerals to cost less and mean more – family by family – community by community seems a good way to start.

www.themodernfuneral.com
brightondeathforum.co.uk

An interview with Victoria Melody for *The Stage*

Your unusual performance practice has seen you immerse yourself in different worlds – whether that's beauty pageants or northern soul dance. What inspired you to take this approach to your work?

In the past I have immersed myself into the worlds of pigeon racing, northern soul dancing, championship dog show handling, beauty pageantry, the human hair industry and most lately for *Ugly Chief* I became a funeral director. I became an active participant and a physical embodiment of the people I was hanging around with in order to take part in their rituals as research for my work.

Rather than recording, documenting and commenting on Britain's clubs and tribes, I become a member and metamorphosise myself in the process. I shine a light on different cultures – but from within the inner sanctums rather than from the outside.

My signature style of creating this type of ethnographic work comes from my early attempts of trying to capture accurate portrayals of various subcultures. I found that my subjects would freeze when they were under the microscopic lens of the camera. Off camera people would reveal more of themselves. We would be laughing and joking and then I would press record and they would freeze. I learnt that if I join in and the camera was focused on me then my subjects were more at ease. By taking part people reveal more of themselves and their customs because you are part of the pack.

Part of the humour comes from me adrift in other people's worlds, worlds where I don't initially seem like I belong. I am passionate about other people's passions, communities see that and they want to share their information with me. I have a genuine interest in what people are doing. I lap up things that may seem domestic and banal, the correct way to wash a hearse may seem dull to some but to me it is an insight into how other people think.

My parents are antique dealers, they really care about the pieces they collect. They are custodians who want to preserve antiques and their provenance. They want to keep the stories of the objects alive. They worry about antiques not being in fashion anymore and that they will end up on the skip with their stories lost forever. I've inherited that need to preserve but rather than antiques my obsession is with the traditions and routines of Britain's subcultures.

How has it been performing and working with your father on Ugly Chief?

Really annoying. Dads generally don't take direction well from their daughters. Also dad isn't a performer he's never performed from a script on stage before. He hasn't had to memorise big chunks of information since he was at school nearly 60 years ago. Generating material for the show was the most fun part. We reminisced and told each other stories, we looked for similarities. We listened to CDs looking for the music for the show. We even visited New Orleans to research how different cultures deal with death.

The problems began after we had the script. There needed to be some level of rigour in order to hit lighting, film and music cues and, most importantly, for the story to be coherent. There is room for improvisation in all my shows hence my choice to work with my dog in Major Tom and my dad in Ugly Chief. It was important to have a scene in the show where dad is completely in his comfort zone valuing antiques from the audience. We really see him and he is always entertaining and it's weird, in a good way, to see a guy from the TV doing an Antiques Roadshow-style valuation during a live theatre show. The tricky part was getting dad to stick to the script. He's never had to do anything like this before. He's a loose cannon who is not used to being told what to do. Every member of my family said they were worried for my career when we announced we were going to be collaborating together. We've had loads of arguments because he kept refusing to learn his lines. He just wanted to go out there and wing it. Unfortunately his pay offs are never great enough when he goes off on a tangent with a meandering story. It took strategies to make this new working relationship succeed and a huge amount of patience.

This is no joke. At one point he even gave me a show rider consisting of his own dressing room with shower, fresh towels, sparkling bottled water, chicken curry or chicken salad brought to his dressing room. We are a small touring company not the RSC, he will be lucky if he gets a toilet cubicle to get changed in and a tub of Pringles.

I think what I am most proud of with this show is it is an exact replica of our real relationship off stage. The show deals with bigger topics and themes than our mundane arguments over who is making the tea. But this show exactly sums up the essence of this father and daughter's relationship. Identical warts and all.

How has training to be a funeral director, as part of the research for this show, changed your perspective on death?

I found working as a funeral director invigorating. This was a strange emotion to feel and it took me a while to understand the reasons why. It's because it helped me to understand my mortality. It's once you have a greater sense of your mortality that you can really start to live your life.

That's why the funeral directors I met do these amazing things on the side. I met an adrenaline junkie cyclist; a world famous chicken fancier; Howard, who worked at the crematorium, races against horses – not on horses but against them. At first I thought they did this to escape the horrors of the job but later I understand that it's because they want to embrace intense experiences of life.

Working in funeral homes made me realise that once you're gone, you're gone it doesn't matter what happens to your body. The funeral is for the living; it is designed to help you mourn. But there is a real market in guilt. An aim of the show is to break the taboo around talking about death. If we talked about it in advance then we could plan more meaningful ceremonies that don't cost the earth and that better reflect the life of the deceased. There is a positive death movement here and in the USA that is really pushing to demystify the funeral process therefore empowering the people left behind to make more informed decisions about what happens to their loved ones. The funeral industry is having to change as people are starting to demand more than the one size fits all generic funeral. The funeral directors I worked with were scrupulous and kind and were generous in helping me to research for this show. They want to work towards helping to make the industry more transparent. But there are accounts of funeral directors capitalising on people's emotional state. It's hard to make decisions when you are at your lowest emotionally – and it can end up costing. The average cost of a funeral in the UK is £3700.

In *Ugly Chief* dad and I write his eulogy together. Not only was it cathartic but it has been one of the most bonding experiences we've ever had. I'm not saying that this is for everyone. But I do think it's a shame that the best speeches are kept for after we've gone and that we don't get to hear them. I think we could be onto something here with the concept of living funerals. If there is a party with all my loved ones telling their favourite stories about me then I want to be there, alive!

Has creating this show given you inspiration for your next subject?

No way! This is the most ambitious project I have ever worked on. It's a 90-minute show with a live band on stage, with eight of us on the road. It's an emotionally challenging show in addition to working alongside a demanding dad. Normally I am researching a new show by now but this one has been so draining that I haven't been able to think of anything else. That's a good sign though; it means I think it's worth the effort.

Production Credits

This is the script from the premiere of *Ugly Chief* at Battersea Art Centre from 31st October 2017 to the 18th November. Vic hopes Mike has learnt his lines by now.

Vic: Victoria Melody

Mike: Mike Melody

The Band: Gemma Storr, Kieran Rafferty, Steve Pretty and James Gow

Written and Conceived by Victoria Melody

Writing Credits Mike Melody and John Gordillo

Director – John Gordillo

Designer – Lucy Bradridge

Musical Director and Original Music – Tom Parkinson

Lighting Designer and Production Manager – Sean

Assistant Stage Manager – Rebecca Hitchcox

Photographer – Hugo Glendinning

Produced by Farnham Maltings

With Thanks

Margaret Melody, Rosie Powell, Martha Oakes, Sue Lancashire, Richard Dufty, Paul Hodson, all at Baglan Funeral Home, Tora at the Modern Funeral, Gavin Stride, Fiona Baxter, Sarah Wilson-White, Janice Brittain, Steph Richardson, Hot 8 Brass Band and Tru Thoughts Records, Tom Brooks at Inter Vivos, Cherice Harrison-Nelson, Markeith Tero, Mitch Mitchinson and Georgina Millett.

Commissioned and developed at New Wolsey Theatre, Farnham Maltings, Battersea Arts Centre and Attenborough Centre for the Creative Arts. Supported by The Point Eastleigh, The Spire, The Marlborough, National Performance Network, and Unity Theatre Trust. Supported using public funding by the National Lottery through Arts Council England. Originally seeded by house with The Old Market.

Team Biographies

Victoria Melody – Performer

Victoria Melody is an award-winning British artist with a background in fine art. She makes theatrical shows, performance interventions and films mainly about Britain's pastimes, passions and tribes. Fascinated by anthropology, she immerses herself into communities and becomes an active participant in their rituals as research for her work.

In the past she has become a pigeon racer, northern soul dancer, championship dog handler, beauty queen, funeral director and police officer.

Victoria has presented her work nationally and internationally at venues including Soho Theatre, Bristol Old Vic, Battersea Arts Centre, Summerhall (Edinburgh Festival Fringe), Cherry Lane Theatre (New York), Virginia Art Festival, Push Festival (Canada), Aarhus Festival (Denmark) and Brisbane Festival (Australia).

Victoria is based in Brighton and is produced by Farnham Maltings.

victoriamelody.com

Mike Melody – Performer

Mike Melody is an antiques dealer. Many will know him as a TV Antiques expert on shows like *Dickinson's Real Deal* and *Secret Dealers*. For the last 40 years Mike and his wife Margaret have run a successful antiques business based in the North of England.

mikemelodyantiques.com

John Gordillo – Director

John Gordillo is an award-winning Comedian who has directed shows by the Comedian Eddie Izzard and was the host and co-creator of *The RDA* (Recommended Daily Allowance), a daily late-night topical comedy talk show, which played heavily with the conventions of the genre. The show ran for 60 episodes until BBC Choice was rebranded as BBC Three.

He has also worked extensively as script editor/director for other comedians including Scott Capurro, Seann Walsh, Josh Widdicombe, Shappi Khorsandi, Dara Ó Briain, Paul Chowdhry, Michael Mcintyre, Mark Steel and Reginald D Hunter. In 2013, he directed the live tour, DVD and TV versions of *Hunter's Live: In the Midst of Crackers*.

In 2014, he produced and co-directed the second series of *Freewheeling with Ross Noble* for Dave TV. In 2015, he directed the live DVD *Dylan Moran: Off the Hook*. He is currently trying to get an independent feature script he has written off the ground.

johngordillo.co.uk

Tom Parkinson – Musical Director and Original Music

Tom Parkinson is a composer and sound designer, working primarily in an interdisciplinary context. He has made the music for over sixty dance and theatre productions in twenty countries. Regular collaborators include theatre-makers Bryony Kimmings and Sharon Smith and choreographers Keren Levi and Ivgi&Greben.

He has worked with/at the National Theatre (UK), the National Theatre of Tunisia, the National Dance Company of Korea, Scottish Ballet, Complicite, the Young Vic, Prague Chamber Ballet, the Royal Opera House, Holland Festival, Julidans (Amsterdam), Phoenix Dance Theatre (Leeds), Provincial Dance Theatre Yekaterinburg (Russia) and Forest Fringe, amongst many others.

He is currently studying for a PhD in composition at Royal Holloway.

tomparkinson.org

Lucy Bradridge – Designer

Lucy Bradridge has designed all Spymonkey shows to date: *Stiff, Cooped, Zumanity, Bless, Moby Dick, Love in* and *Oedipussy*, as well as the collaborations *Spookshow, Every Last Trick* and *Mrs Hudson's Christmas Corker*.

Lucy has collaborated on numerous occasions with clown director Cal Mccrystal, including Alan Ayckboure's *Mr Whatnot* at Royal & Derngate, *Bubonic Play* and *Hello Dalai* for Piggy Nero, *Between a Rock and a Hard Place* for Cambridge Footlights, and Fitzrovia Radio's *Dracula* at Mercury Colchester.

Design credits include *Autoboosh* for the Mighty Boosh; clown costume design for Cirque Du Soleil's *Varekai* and *Zumanity*; *Heroes* for company fz; *moonjourney* by Alice Lowe; New Art Club's *Trials of Hercules*; *Gloves On* and *Our Dancing Feet* for Ragroof Players.

Television credits include *Orcadia*, *A Comedy Lab*, and *The Last Chancers*, a comedy series both for Channel4.

Film credits include *The Wild and Wycked World* of Brian Jones; *Out of Water* and *Queen Bee*.

James Gow – Musician

James is a multi-instrumentalist and composer with a BA in Music from the School of Oriental and African Studies, University of London. He is a regular musician with Kneehigh (*The Flying Lovers of Vitebsk*, *Dead Dog in a Suitcase (and other love songs)*, *Tristan & Yseult* and *Brief Encounter*). Outside of the theatre he can occasionally be seen in several bands including genre-hopping jazz-fusion group Lunch Money, Cocos Lovers and others from the Smugglers Records music scene, Eleven Magpies, and alongside the multi-instrumental folk trio Three Cane Whale.

soundcloud.com/flamespow

Steve Pretty – Musician

Steve Pretty does mostly performance, music composition, arranging and production, and sometimes photography and writing. He runs the Hackney Colliery Band, a 9-piece modern brass band playing rock, jazz, electronica and soul. He's done two 60-minute solo shows which were really well reviewed at the Edinburgh Fringe. He does some comedy and is resident music bloke at the Alternative Comedy Memorial Society and for Robin Ince and Brian Cox's shows. In 2015, he co-created the kids show *Annabelle's Skirtingboard Adventure* with all-round comedy and writing legend Howard Read, which was described as 'a show which is unlikely to be outdone on originality anywhere else on the Fringe' by The Scotsman.

stevepretty.com

Gemma Storr – Musician

Multi instrumentalist Gemma is a London based composer and musician specialising in collaborative works for public spaces.

As founder and MD of the Minds Ear Orchestra she is interested in breaking down traditional audience–performer–composer barriers.

She is mostly inventing giant musical toys at Trinity Laban Conservatoire of Music and Dance, where she has been awarded the Headley fellowship to explore her practice.

Notorious for her rowdy stage shows, she loves pop music above all else and is currently performing with post apocalypse rock-o-nauts This Mighty Fever, and all girl bluegrass group The Jolenes.

mindsearorchestra.com

Kieran Rafferty – Musician

Kieran is a musician, writer and performer. As well as working in bands and as a solo performer in the UK, Europe and on national radio, he writes and performs with comedian John Whale – they are currently working on their Edinburgh 2018 show. He has written music and/or words for E4, Penguin books, and teaches creative practice at Newcastle University, where he recently completed his PhD thesis on popular song structure in early 20th century New York only slightly later than requested.

kieranrafferty.com

Rebecca Hitchcox – Assistant Stage Manager

Rebecca Hitchcox is the Assistant Stage Manager. She is a postgraduate student currently on the Theatre Production Arts Postgraduate Diploma course at Mountview Academy of Theatre Arts (specialising in Stage Management). Before this, she completed a BA in Drama & Theatre Studies at Royal Holloway University of London. Recently, she just finished working as an ASM on Trouble In Mind at the Print Room at the Coronet. She continues to work as a Tech Assistant for Blackshaw Theatre Company with the various shows they put on, the most recent being their Scare Slam at London Horror Festival.

Farnham Maltings – Producer

Farnham Maltings is a cultural organisation that works with artists and communities of South East England to encourage the most people to make the best art they can. We believe that the arts help us to make sense of the world, bring people together and articulate new ideas. By encouraging people to participate in the arts, as audiences and makers, we will foster a healthier, happier and safer contemporary Britain.

We are curious about how we make and build an audience for contemporary theatre. We support a network of 220 venues across the region, organise a biennial showcase of new English performance for an international audience, produce a stable of independent theatre companies and are working to diversify the makers and audience for the arts.

farnhammaltings.com

ACT ONE

SCENE 1
PRE-SHOW

BAND playing instrumental New Orleans Jazz as the audience enter. The BAND are stage left and wearing black, they are talking amongst themselves like they are playing in the background of a busy bar. Stage left there is a minimalist lectern. Centre stage back there in a curtain rail, the curtains are heavy grey fabric, they are closed.

VIC enters stage. MUSIC stops. She is wearing a black tail coat, white shirt, pin stripe skirt and black sensible shoes.

She looks like a traditional funeral director. Her delivery is direct to the audience, she is friendly and jovial.

VIC
Hello, thank you for coming my name is Victoria Melody. Before we start tonight's show I wanted to let you in on a few things.

Now normally I make shows on my own but this time I'm doing a show with my DAD! And therein lies the problem.

Some of you might know dad, he's an antique dealer and he used to be a regular on TV's Dickinson's Real Deals. But he was thrown off that show for yawning at David Dickinson... and for refusing to apologise. He was transferred to another programme – Secret Dealers. Any fans of that in?

Did you know that Dad's episodes of Secret Dealers are the most repeated...according to him.

Now in 2012 the doctors diagnosed dad with motoneuron's disease. They gave him less than five years to live.

He asked me to organise his funeral. So I looked into it and I couldn't believe how expensive funerals were.

VIC *(Cont'd.)*
So I started doing some research and the more I found out about the funeral industry the more fascinating it seemed – so I decided to train as a funeral director.
    (Sarcastic.)
Which is the obvious way to deal with feelings of grief.

So I come back from my training and dad gives me some news...

Dad do you want to come and explain for yourself? Ladies & Gentleman, please welcome my dad Mike Melody.

    MIKE walks onto stage. He's wearing a checked shirt over a pair of red chinos. The shirt is a bit creased and his long hair looks a bit disheveled. He looks very casually dressed compared to VIC. He is cantankerous but has a cheeky glint in his eye.

MIKE
Hello – as you can see I'm still here.
I wasn't allowed on till now cause our Vic said it would spoil the narrative arc, or something like that. I'm not a thespian.
    (To VIC.)
You've only been on 30 seconds – we could have come out together – it's not like I didn't hear what you were saying...

VIC
(Ignoring his grumpy remark.)
Anyway, so dad gets diagnosed in 2012...

MIKE
2011

VIC
2012 I've got proof...

    PAUSE.

this is why I need to do this bit because the show wont make sense unless people understand that you keep changing your mind about everything.

    Back to audience.

So I go off and become a funeral director – then what happened
dad?

MIKE
(This is amazing news, he's enthusiastic.)
Well, AFTER I was diagnosed with Motor Neuron by this clown
called – Dr F … Vic says I'm not allowed to say his name
for legal reasons. I WAS TERRIFIED – I made a will, gave up
drinking, changed my whole life.

I had two years of being poked and prodded by doctors.
They electrocuted me.

VIC
(Sarcastic.)
But did they really electrocute you?

MIKE
I'm telling you they put bloody things on your hands to check
your nerves and they all sit there laughing saying does that
hurt? No.

Anyhow I googled motor neuron like you do and **I wasn't
getting any weaker, there was no physical deterioration.**
So I plucked up the courage and I went back. And I said can
you have another look. And this Doctor F, you know the type
pinstripe suit, bald head.
He had another look and he said you know what you don't
happen to have motor neuron.

I jumped up in the air, not far because of my dodgy leg.
I couldn't believe it – **!!! I was going to live – Wa hayy!! – …**
But what a bastard so **UP YOURS DOCTOR FLETCHER!**

VIC
DAD IT'S ILLEGAL TO SAY HIS NAME!!!
    (To audience.)
So for one year we thought we were going to lose dad at any
minute.
Then the doctors realised they had made a mistake and
misdiagnosed him.
    (BEAT.)
People always want to know what is wrong with you then?

(To audience.)
If you google Mike Melody the first three things that come up are Mike Melody antique dealer, Mike Melody's daughter *(me)* and Mike Melody has he had a stroke?

MIKE
I've got a trapped nerve in the vertebrae in the top of my neck. It's stuck in my central nervous system. It's semi paralysed my arm and my leg. They can't operate because if it goes wrong there's a 75% chance I will be disabled from the neck down. So apart from having a limp and a gammy arm (shakes arm) I'm perfect.

VIC
So once we knew that dad wasn't going to pass...

MIKE
What do you mean, pass?

VIC
Oh, yes! I was taught this – when you're a funeral director, it's better to use euphemisms for when a person...
(She can't say it, she has been too well-trained.)
...transitions...
(Off his blank look.)
You know: goes to a better place...falls asleep...

MIKE
DIES!! Just say I was going to die! Nothing to fear from the word, Vic.

VIC
(Ignoring him; to audience.)
Anyway... I'd already planned his funeral...
...and already become this fully trained funeral director.

So when dad was given the all clear, I thought: well I've done the research why don't we collaborate and make a show about the whole thing, and it would be a living funeral. Because after all a funeral is like a...really sad theatre show!

And anyway why are the best speeches kept for after we've gone? So I asked dad and he said:

MIKE
Well obviously, yes: I'm here, aren't I?

VIC
And this is where the problems started.

Please meet the band.

> *The BAND play underscore the following conversation with Green Onions by Booker T. & the M.G.'s. VIC walks over and introduces GEMMA, KIERAN, STEVE and JAMES. They all play multi instruments. Keyboard is played by GEMMA.*

This is Gemma her dad holds the 1972 Guinness World record for going to all the tube stations. Her parents once bought a house from the drummer of the rock band deep purple. Every single room was painted purple.

This is Kieran his dad was a Costa Brava pool tournament champion. He wore a leather jacket and listened to Status Quo in his old, yellow Rover SD1, which looked like a cross between a Porsche and a rusty banana. Kieran thought he was unbelievably cool.

This is James when he was a baby his dad lost an eye in an accident. His dad took advantage of the situation by dressing up James as a parrot, putting him on his shoulder and going to a fancy dress party dressed as a pirate.

This is Steve his dad is an actor who was playing a sea captain in a panto. At the same time Steve was caught up in the 2004 Boxing Day tsunami and was unable to get in touch with his parents for nearly 10 days and was reported dead by the Daily Mail. His dad still had to perform and deliver the line 'oh woe, oh woe, oh woe is me, for my son is lost to the killer sea' for 12 shows a week.

And the band are here because of one of the most important scenes in my life. Because I work in theatre I see my life in scenes now...

They are here because dad asked me to remember the music for his funeral when I was seven years old.

I'd sit with him in his music room (which was really a stock room with a CD player). He'd play me CD's of his favorite music – our house was chaotic. So these moments when dad shone his light on me were special. My friends were listening to Kylie & Jason and I was listening to Sam & Dave.

I'll never forget the day, when dad, smoking one of his 80 cigarettes a day! – that's eight fags an hour!! He turned to me and said: "Our Vic, I love this song. It's up to you to remember this is the music I want at my funeral. Because, our Vic, I don't think anyone else will remember." It's a responsibility I have taken seriously my whole life.

Takes handwritten list out of pocket. Gives to MIKE, he scrutinizes it in-between listening to the music.

And I've still got that list. And so because we are giving dad a living funeral. I hired the band to play dad's funeral music. Song one please.

BAND stop playing Green Onions and play OPENING BARS OF WALKING TO NEW ORLEANS

VIC *(Cont'd.)*
Thank you. – That was WALKING TO NEW ORLEANS by Fats Domino. SONG TWO ...

BAND PLAY OPENING BARS OF DOWN IN THE VALLEY.

VIC *(Cont'd.)*
Thank you. That was DOWN IN THE VALLEY by Solomon Burke. SONG THREE please...

BAND PLAY OPENING BARS OF NEW ORLEANS by Gary U.S. Bonds.

VIC *(Cont'd.)*
Thank you. That was New Orleans by Gary U.S. Bonds. They are brilliant aren't they?

They've really worked hard – we've got thirteen of these songs. Only...dad – you want to tell them?

MIKE
(To audience.)
I have absolutely no recollection of asking Vic to remember the songs for my funeral.
Don't know what she's on about. And if I did give her that list, one song I would have definitely put in there would have been For Ever More by Jesse Yawn and that's not on here, so I can't see how this conversation ever happened.
(To BAND.)
Do FOREVER MORE by Jesse Yawn.

The BAND are stumped. He tries to teach it to them.

MIKE *(Cont'd.)*
See? They don't know it. So I never told you to remember my funeral music.

VIC
(To audience.)
This is typical of dad.

VIC *(Cont'd.)*
THE ONLY REASON WE GOT A BAND IN IS SO THEY COULD PLAY THESE SONGS!!!
(Thrown away.)
Now they're going to have to be here to give the scenes emotional depth.

VIC *(Cont'd.)*
Gemma, Kieran, Steve and James

THE BAND
(Worried.)
Yes?

VIC
Do you think you can just jam along with the scenes and give them emotional depth? Just play whatever you think will work. You've already gone to the effort maybe squeeze in some of the songs you've learnt...if it's appropriate.

THE BAND
(Looking at each other, checking if it's OK.)
Errr yeah we can do that. Sounds good...

> The BAND talk amongst themselves.

> As VIC tries to speak the BAND start playing something a bit weird. VIC looks a bit nervous like her request may have been a mistake.

VIC
Then there's the name of this show. Dad told me that our surname, Melody, which is our real name, is Gaelic and it means Ugly Chief. And I thought, that's the perfect title for the show. So I went away and designed the flyers and posters and sent them out and it turns out Melody doesn't mean Ugly Chief. Melody means...

> BAND abruptly stop.

VIC (Cont'd.)
"tune".

MIKE
It's true. I got one of those 48 hour free trials on Ancestry dot whatever it's called.

VIC
Just because it's from the internet it doesn't mean it's true... So now you've got the backstory we can finally begin the show.

> This bit all fast paced. GEMMA decides to play church organ music. An antique chair is brought out for MIKE, he sits down. VIC put's on a top hat and has a funeral directors silver handled walking stick, she opens curtains using a pulley system.

> BAND Ushers KIERAN, JAMES & STEVE and REBECCA the Assistant Stage Manager bring in the coffin – Feet First. They walk it past MIKE. MIKE pulls a face of disgust. BAND bow to coffin once laid down. They remove the flowers and coffin lid, bowing to everyone and everything. VIC stands

directly in front of coffin. BAND take their places and join in with GEMMA underscoring the next scene in a song that is probably a bit too sombre.

LIGHTS FIND:

SCENE 2
BEGINNING OF SHOW – FUNERAL DIRECTING PART ONE

VIC
It's REALLY interesting stuff – the way we deal with death in Britain and the taboos, around it. Plus I take responsibility very seriously. If I was going to be in charge of dad's funeral then I needed to find out everything about funerals. So I decided to train as a funeral director.

VIC walks over to the coffin. She erects a projection screenthat's been concealed inside the coffin. She does this slowly with comic timing as she speaks.

VIC *(Cont'd.)*
But I couldn't find any local traditional funeral homes who'd train me – then I watched this TV series called "A Very Welsh Undertaking." On there was a man called Gareth he seemed a good character with a sense of humour. I called him up. He's got this great attitude to death and he's up for letting people know what happens when the curtain closes at the crematorium – plus he knew my dad off the TV. He said he'd train me and that I seemed
(Stretches neck and says to MIKE.)
a very interesting and intelligent person. Because that's what people think about me.
(To audience.)
I was nervous about learning to be a funeral director. I was on my way to a funeral home in deepest Southern Wales with a suitcase and a mind that didn't know what to expect.

I didn't know what I was going to find, what the people were going to be like, how I was going to deal with death. I didn't even know if there was going to be a food shop.

I was off to Baglan funeral home in Port Talbot.

NEW MUSIC playing: gentle slow and sweet music. It's a contrast to VIC's quite graphic, odd and sometimes disturbing descriptions. VIC tries to subtly nod to the BAND to get them to change it. They don't see it.

Projected onto SCREEN: PORT TALBOT & BAGLAN FUNERAL HOME MONTAGE. Clips of the exterior and interior of the funeral home. Image of Gareth with his hearses. Video clip of VIC trying to position all the funeral directors from Baglan's Funeral Home for a photo outside the funeral home.

Clip of VIC doing all her duties as a funeral director – stapling material inside a coffin, wearing a top hat whilst etching out letters onto a plaque, screwing a plaque into the coffin lid, arranging flowers in the funeral home and driving the hearse.

VIC (Cont'd.)
Gareth the owner picked me up from the train station, immaculately dressed with gleaming white teeth he got on the cheap in Turkey. He said "Hello Vicky, get in the car".

The funeral home is the grandest building in Baglan complete with mock Georgian pillars. On site, they have a viewing room, mortuary, they do embalming: everything!

They gave me the nickname Fergie because my hair's a bit red. And... Neil Kinnock. But I liked them a lot.

Now Funeral directing is not a role I ever imagined myself in. Although I used to be a Goth. But I'm a naturally happy person. So I just used to really annoy the other Goths.

After being at the funeral home a week, nobody died, the staff blamed me. Normally there's about 20 funerals. They called me the jinx. Apart from I think I'm the opposite of a jinx because I'm prolonging people's lives.

Then one day, Gareth said, "c'mon Vicky...get in the mortuary".

I'd told them I wasn't squeamish but I lied. I'm a vegetarian because looking at dead flesh makes me sick, I can't stand the sight of blood. I can just about eat a fish if it's covered in sauce and looks like a vegetable.

I put on a white coat and latex gloves. The staff were all like, "go on then Vicky, get your hands dirty!" And I could feel all their eyes on me...it was like a test. They wanted to see if I was up to the job.

VIC steps back into place so curtains will close around her.

I picked up a man's arm and they said 'be careful'. He'd been dead a while his skin was decomposing, he's got something called skin slip. They said be careful because if I pull too hard the skin will come off his hand like a glove.

BAND close curtains closing VIC in with the coffin. MIKE signals to the BAND they help him put on a STRIPE BOATING JACKET, with reading glasses in the pocket. This is the same jacket he wore on his TV programs. They go back and play an antiques show type theme.

MUSIC UP: MIKE'S ANTIQUES THEME

MIKE from his chair says

MIKE
Christ this is miserable... ALL RIGHT, MY TURN NOW, close those curtains!!!!

LIGHTS UP.

SCENE 3
ANTIQUES VALUATION

The BAND help set a table DOWNSTAGE CENTRE and gather up items from the audience. MIKE stands centre stage by table.

MIKE
Well that was bloody depressing.

Vic and I struck a deal that she could do her miserable research if I could have some fun... So lets lighten things up.

We're going to do some live antiques valuation.

MIKE (Cont'd.)
If I like anything enough, I'll buy it and we'll hear MIKE'S EXCITEMENT THEME.

35

The BAND look a bit scared and jam something exciting with trumpets.

MIKE values antiques and is funny and witty, he describes in detail what the items look like. The following is one example from a show we did in Brighton.

Gemma has collected two porcelain figurines from the audience and put them on the table.

MIKE *(Cont'd.)*
I think I know what these are.
(To AUDIENCE MEMBER.)

Are they Royal Doulton?

AUDIENCE MEMBER
Yes.

MIKE
(Pleased with himself.)
Wa, hay. Who's a boy?

He turns the figurines upside down and studies them.

Let me tell you the problem with Royal Doulton. They used to make all these figurines and other bits, they did Toby jugs as well. They cornered the market, the early editions sold for thousands.

He picks up one of the figurines.

Something like this would have sold for 600/700 quid. Unfortunately Doulton got taken over and they thought clever idea we will do re-strikes. So these figures are remodels from the originals. Sorry about that. Their nice things, but there not worth a carrot. I hate to say it. Did you pay a lot for them?

AUDIENCE MEMBER
Oh no! I've got a hundred of them. They were left to me by my great aunty Margaret.

DAD
(Amused.)

Well have a look through them, if there's any grubby looking ones. They are the ones worth money. Send me some photos of them I might even buy them.

Well I've had a nice easy life of it. Thank you! All right and now we're going to go back to Vic for more uplifting stories...

BAND remove the table and open curtains revealing VIC. MIKE walks off UPSTAGE.

LIGHTS DARKEN TO:

SCENE 4
FUNERAL DIRECTING PART TWO

MUSIC: BAND PLAY SOMBRE FUNERAL PARLOUR THEME

She wears WHITE COAT & LATEX GLOVES.

VIC
The mouth is open when you die. You sew it closed. It means putting cotton thread through the nose and hooking it with a needle through the gums and tying it. I sewed a mouth shut. It's very unnatural trying to get somebody to look natural.

At the crematorium as soon as one family have gone out the back door. Then there is another family coming through the front door. It's like a conveyor belt.

I go down to the basement with the cremulators – which are like massive pizza ovens. The coffin goes in and burns straight away.

The wood goes white with the heat and it's like a shell cracking and you see the body – like a dinosaur being born out of an egg. The last thing to go is your brain, as it's so well encased in your skull. The ashes and bones and a metal hip replacement come through a shoot into a bucket.

I went to the crematorium. I watched a body burn and I found it invigorating!

That time at Baglan funeral home is one of the best times in my life and that is so strange!

MIKE *(Off stage.)*
All right that's enough... No... I'm going on...

> *MIKE comes on. He can't take it anymore...but VIC tries to keep on with it...*

VIC
But when you are seeing it like that, it's not a body, it's not a person anymore. You are seeing something before your eyes turning into organic matter...it's not until you understand your mortality that you can really start to live your life.

MIKE
What's the point of all this?
Nobody wants to see this...
> *(He keeps trying to get her attention.)*

> *Finally he stops her.*

MIKE *(Cont'd.)*
What are you doing?

VIC
I'm just telling them about my training...

MIKE
This is Vic's problem – she goes off and she gets lost in the research...

Who cares about this – where's my LIVING funeral?
Get on with it...

VIC
Aright! It's coming up, it's literally the next scene,
Let's set the stage for dad's funeral...here put this on.

> *She gets lectern and gives him an old jacket that's split down the back.*

MIKE
What's this?

VIC
It's what you would have worn at your funeral.

MIKE

I haven't worn this for years – And when I wore it, it was only
for seeing the bank manager and going to court.

(Showing the back.)

And why's it got a great big slit down the back?

VIC

(To audience.)

Ah...well, actually...

(Becoming all nerdy and excited.)

...this is very interesting. It's something from my field work
at the Funeral Director's. When families bring clothes to the
funeral home, they usually bring suits for the men but they're
from a time when they were younger and thinner. So we have
to cut them down the back to give the illusion that it still
fits. There's all this stuff that goes on behind the scenes at a
funeral home. It's fascinating!

MIKE

Grunt.

VIC

OK!... So I will now deliver the eulogy I was trained to give.

Getting top hat and tail coat and putting it on.

Somebody asked me what a eulogy was. According to the CO-
OP how to write a eulogy brochure "a eulogy is a speech in
praise of someone who has died that's meant to capture the
essence of a person."

Now here is the genuine eulogy I wrote for dad if he really
would have died.

MIKE

Get on with it!

SCENE 5
CHAPEL

Hint of organ music. MIKE sits on stage in a heavy antique chair that resembles a wooden throne. VIC walks to the lectern. MIKE heckles. A photomontage of MIKE through the years from baby to now is projected.

VIC
We are gathered here today to celebrate the life of Michael Anthony Dominic Melody. M A D, MAD Melody. Also known as Smed, Mickey in the antique trade and to my sisters and me as Dad. We give thanks for his life.

Mike was son to Martin who was a signalman in the army and Marjorie who unfortunately died when Mike was a young boy.

Mike was clever and passed his 11+ when he was nine.

MIKE
Should have called it the 11 minus

VIC
He was awarded a scholarship at St Joseph's college. An all-boys school run by the Christian brothers...

MIKE
... Christian buggers more like...

VIC
Mike left unscathed and thanks the fact that he was not an attractive child.

MIKE
I had a hairy arse.

VIC
In school the richer boys teased Mike for his tatty second hand clothes. He was disruptive in class, even in his favorite subject, art. Asked to do the sign writing for the school play, there were audible gasps on opening night when the curtain drew back revealing a shop belonging to Mr B. Ugger and F. Uck and Sons.

MIKE
I also did S. Hithead.

VIC
He was kicked out of school. His teacher said that the best he could hope for was to become a tramp.

His father was strict and not always the most loving and compassionate. When Mike came home one night at 16 after a drunken night out, he opened the door to see his bed being pushed down the stairs by his dad. Mike picked up the suitcase and hit the streets. There were various jobs: he measured rulers, sold faulty vending machines, beefburgers on Blackpool beach and fake meat to Indian restaurants who then sold it on as real meat.

In the 1960s Mike joined a band. despite the fact he couldn't sing or play an instrument...

MIKE
... Not true!

VIC
(To MIKE.)
OK, what instrument did you play?

MIKE
The organ

VIC
(To audience.)
None of us have ever seen him play the organ. Mum went to see his band once and he was sat on the top of a speaker blowing bubbles. The original Bez.

    Back to eulogy.

They were called The Jinx Soul band. When the band were "on tour", five miles away he met my mum Margaret. Margie was the manager of Nanna's caravan site. Mum had just come out of a relationship with Keith Harris of Orville the Duck fame. Mike was always jealous of Harris's television success.

MIKE
Oi! I bloody wasn't!

VIC
Mike and Margaret fell in love. They got married in a ceremony that cost £1.50.

MIKE
12 quid! We had a horse shoe wedding cake...it was half price because there's less cake.

VIC
They bought a big dilapidated fully furnished house in Chester. When they needed extra money they would sell the furniture on a market stall. And this is how Melody's Antique Galleries – "purveyors of seriously good antiques" was born.

The 80s were good, the antique trade was booming. Mike fulfilled a lifelong dream of owning a Mercedes.

Soon after he crashed it into a cow.

One day, intoxicated, at an auction, Mike accidentally bought a house. This is the house my sisters and I grew up in.

I had an interesting upbringing. And Mike wasn't always easy to live with. Just like him I hit the streets with a suitcase at 16. But eventually we reconciled. As the saying goes: blood is thicker than water.

He was an eternal optimist, he didn't see a problem, he saw an opportunity. When I had to have surgery on my spine, he said look on the bright side if it goes wrong, you will be the first in the family with one of those blue disabled badges.

Mike was an eccentric character who will not be easily forgotten – a one of a kind.

He wouldn't want us sat here, upset. He would say something like "Don't be sad because I am happy. I've lived a life of extremes, never a dull moment."

We will now take a moment to reflect on and remember Mike while we sing one of his favorite songs... Please can you stand and open your hymn sheets to page 2.

The congregation (audience) stand and sing a dirge hymnal version of Soul Man by Sam and Dave backed by GEMMA playing church organ. The rest of the BAND help in leading the singing. It sounds awful and nobody knows how to sing the first verse after the chorus.

I'm a soul man
I'm a soul man
I'm a soul man
I'm a soul man

Coming to you on a dusty road
Good loving, I got a truck load
And when you get it, you got something
So don't worry, 'cause I'm coming

I'm a soul man

MIKE gets out of his chair, he can't stand it anymore.

MIKE
Stop it! Stop it,
(*To the ORGANIST.*)
STOP PLAYING!
(*To the audience.*)
Sit down, sit down. Can I talk now?
Get some lights on. – This is bloody dreadful! Bloody farce.
Was that meant to be Sam and Dave?
You've just butchered one of my favorite songs...

LIGHTS UP. Everyone sits. Once he has the room...

This is exactly why I don't like funerals. None of this is me, why not ask me what I want?

I'll tell you what really gets my goat at funerals is people saying: "*it's what he would have wanted*". What a load of bollocks. If it's what he would have wanted how come he wants exactly the same as every other bastard in a box. This is why all funerals are the same. Nobody wants to talk about death when they're alive so you end up second guessing a corpse and you get this bog standard CO-OP shite that's meant to make the family feel better...as if splashing out on a fancy coffin or getting a bigger hearse means you loved them more. It's a market in guilt...

43

What I'm saying is I'm here.

VIC, BAND AND THE CONGREGATION
You want to give me a living funeral, why not ask me what I want?

> *A BEAT – MIKE looks expectantly at VIC. She turns to the audience and pings off into bouncy narrator mode... VIC busies herself talking whilst getting things.*

VIC
Actually when dad first said this to me, I had to admit he had a good point. Also he was raising a really important question about the way we deal with death.
(BEAT.)
I've arranged quite a few funerals now. I'm a pro. So I thought it would be good to have a scene in the show where I sit down with dad and arrange the funeral he actually wants.

MIKE
Thank you.

VIC
No problem.
(Getting excited again, she asks BAND to help get chairs.)
I've got a proper questionnaire that funeral directors use.

> *She rushes up to get it from the lectern. She gets out a A4 FOLDER and is trying to look official. The BAND set two antique ladder back chairs, centre stage.*

MIKE
(Referring to questionnaire.)
What do you need that for? Why don't you just ask me?

> *VIC ignores him.*

> *LIGHTS CHANGE:*

SCENE 6
FUNERAL PLANNING

VIC pulls up a chair far too close to him.

Tasteful, tuneless organ music plays softly under the scene.

MIKE
What you sitting so close for? Get away.

VIC
Hello, Mr. Melody. I'm sorry for my loss.
(*BEAT.*)
Now, would you like to be buried or cremated?

MIKE
Buried.

VIC
Do you want a religious or...

MIKE
(*Remembering.*)
Oooh – in the back garden. I want to be buried in the garden.

VIC
OK, do you want a religious or non-religious ceremony?

MIKE
Non-religious. Obviously.

VIC
Where would you like the funeral to take place?

MIKE
I want it in a barbecue pit.

VIC
(*VIC looks at audience.*)
A barbecue pit?

MIKE
There's a place in Chester – called the Hickory Smokehouse, great steaks, sawdust on the floor type of place.

VIC
Why?

MIKE
It's what I want.

> *VIC notes it down, finding it weird.*

VIC
Would you like hymns or prayers?

DAD
You know I don't. Also I don't want anyone crying or wearing black.

VIC
Would you like flowers?

MIKE
OK – but nothing that's white. I hate them. They look funereal. Tangerine coloured – Blackpool FC colours.

VIC
Would you like to be viewed?

MIKE
What's that???

VIC
It's when people come to see you.

MIKE
No!

VIC
How would you like your hair and make-up done?

MIKE
Does it matter? I'm not going out on the pull.

VIC
What would you like to wear?

MIKE
Blackpool Football kit.

VIC
What would you like the congregation to wear?

MIKE
Same – tangerine strip.

VIC
Would you like music?

MIKE

Yeah. I want a New Orleans Jazz procession – I want it to be a party, a celebration.

VIC
Do you want an obituary?

MIKE
Yes.

VIC
What publication?

MIKE
Antiques Trade Gazette.

VIC
What do you want it to say?

MIKE
Business as usual. 20% discount.

VIC
What kind of coffin would you like?

ON SCREEN: SLIDES OF COFFINS illustrating what VIC is showing MIKE on stage. BAND plays sale music. Coffin clips and VIC go fast and snappy through this segment. VIC is off book and points to the coffins with her Funeral Director's walking stick. She delivers the prices to the audience.

MIKE heckles these throughout with whatever witticisms he fancies saying on the day. MIKE FINDS THIS STUFF INCREDIBLY GROSS ...

VIC *(Cont'd.)*
Perhaps you might like something from our English Heritage range.

MIKE
You what?

VIC
We have the Buckingham, the Windsor, the Marlborough, the Warwick... all solid oak caskets, with routered panel sides and veneered double mouldings. You may not have lived like a king but you can spend eternity like one.
    (To audience.)
Price only £799.
Or from our Last Supper Range we have the Corpus Christi – a solid oak coffin with the 'Head of Christ' carved into the sides featuring an optional image of the Last Supper on the inside of the lid.
    (To audience.)
These are all real by the way!
Price is £1,899
Or why not treat yourself to... The Promethean? This casket has a 48 oz solid bronze finish with 14-Carat Gold Plated handles. It has a hermetically-sealing lid and a mechanical locking mechanism. The interior is high quality herringbone and has a fully adjustable bed and mattress. It has a reversible pillow and overthrow.
    (To audience.)
Cost is £19,999

MIKE
NEVER – PLEASE VIC!
Just stick me in a bourbon barrel.

VIC
(VIC looks at audience.)
A bourbon barrel?

MIKE
A bourbon barrel – you're bound to find one on Ebay.
All right, got it now? Let's move on...

VIC
(Not listening.)
Do you want the undertaker to walk in front of the hearse?

MIKE
No! Come on, we're finished.

VIC
(Not listening.)
Do you want any of the following? A piper.

MIKE
No.

VIC
A multi-media presentation.

MIKE
No.

VIC
A dove

MIKE
No.

VIC
Blessing tree?

MIKE
What's that? No!

VIC
What kind of food would you like at the wake?

MIKE
Anchovies & pineapples on a stick. For Christ's sake, Vic –
I've said what I want – everyone in tangerine, bourbon barrel,
barbecue pit, New Orleans jazz. That's it. Let's stop now,
it's gone on forever...

VIC
(Relenting, shutting the book.)
OK.

MIKE
And I want you to read the eulogy I wrote.

> *A BEAT.*

VIC
I don't think that's a good idea.

MIKE
Why not?

VIC
Because, it's not very good.
> *(To audience.)*
When we were rehearsing this scene, I asked dad to go away and think about what sort of things he might like included in his eulogy – and 20 mins later he came back and said he'd written it. You can't write a eulogy in 20 mins. You've got to think about it.

MIKE
It's what I want. You're supposed to give me what I want.

VIC
(Reluctant.)
All right…
> *(To audience.)*
We've got to reset the stage for the next bit so let's take a 15-minute break and when we come back, we're going to give dad the exact funeral service he's asked for…
> *(To BAND.)*
Will you play us out please…

> *MIKE and VIC go off. BAND play Fats Domino's WALKING TO NEW ORLEANS.*

> *HOUSE LIGHTS UP.*

> *END OF ACT ONE.*

ACT TWO

AS THE INTERVAL COMES TO A CLOSE ...

The audience return, they are given TANGERINE CLOTHING at the door, while VIC (now in unflattering Blackpool F.C. kit, Orange top, boys white shorts, orange socks pulled up and orange trainers) dutifully decks the stage out in tangerine (football scarves, decorations etc.) She brings out a BBQ, throws sawdust on the floor. The stage is a mess. The lectern is placed on the opposite side of the stage to Act One.

The BAND are warming up and talking. This morphs into a drunken blues.

SCENE 7
DAD'S SELF-WRITTEN FUNERAL & AFTERMATH

HOUSE LIGHTS COME DOWN.

MIKE is wheeled on in a massive bourbon barrel on wheels. He is placed upstage centre in front of the curtains. VIC walks to the lectern. This eulogy is presented lightly and not as formal as before. There is banter between VIC and MIKE.

Preamble from VIC.

VIC
Thanks for coming back for Part Two. Now we do the exact funeral that dad has requested. This is exactly how he would like to be remembered.
  (To MIKE, who is surveying the debris on stage.)
I mean you must be pretty pleased with all this?

MIKE
(Ungrateful.)
Is that BBQ and sawdust meant to be my Hickory BBQ pit?

VIC
(Ignores him.)
And can I just point out how unflattering these football tops are.
You can't tell whose the daughter and whose the dad.

Reading eulogy.
We are gathered here today to celebrate the life of Michael Anthony Dominic Melody. M A D, MAD Melody. Also known as Smed, Mickey in the antique trade and to my sisters and me as Dad. We give thanks for his life.

(Steps away.)
The eulogy I'm about to read is one that dad wrote in 20 mins during rehearsals. These are the exact words he wants read out at his funeral.

(Back to the lectern.)
"All right you lot. So this is a thank you note about my life that sums up the essence of me. Here we go.

I would first like to thank God if there is one for landing me in the British Isles and not in the Gobi desert and being born in the 50s, my parents for helping me get out of the ghetto by insisting on educating me. No problems!!!

Blackpool was my early home and what a great place to observe life in all its formats from the clowns at the circus to the awe inspiring illuminations.

(To MIKE.) Are you being sarcastic about Blackpool's awe inspiring illuminations?

MIKE
No they are a world famous attraction. And will you not interrupt my eulogy!

VIC
...the Seasiders – my football team Blackpool F.C.

> *The BAND start to play Glad All Over by The Dave Clark Five. The BAND are really happy about it and enjoying themselves. It's the Blackpool FC goal song. VIC shoots them a look. MIKE sings along. She motions for them to turn the volumn down for the rest of the eulogy.*

MIKE
(Enthusiastic .)
It's the Blackpool FC goal song. Love it.

VIC
(*Back to reading eulogy.*)
... I have always believed it should be compulsory for everyone to support the football team of where you're from – it should be tattooed on your body. It should be the law.

What if like me you hate football?

MIKE
Well tough luck. Get on with it!

VIC
I had the number one best day of my life – back in 2010 when the Seasiders got into the Premiership – surpasses anything by a barn door.

Onwards to the Merseyside area through work in the mid 60s how lucky could I be! Music, music music!

I joined the obligatory band and by complete accident became immersed in the blues and soul music, wow, lucky or what.

On this journey I met my wife, another lucky coincidence or what?? Many, many, normal developments along the way including a lucky change of career from selling artificial meat for Courtaulds Edible Spun Protein, 10 times flatulence content of baked beans.
(*To MIKE.*)
That's not even a sentence

MIKE
Well it is, makes you fart.

VIC
(*Reading.*)
I failed miserably to antique dealing after a bad car crash.

At this turning point I had two children and eventually had a third. Our Vic being the second.

Antique dealing in the 70s, 80s and 90s gave us a good living but with it came the trappings, money ,cars and drink!!

Fortunately holding it altogether was my dear wife Marg, what a star, don't call me lucky!! Thank you.

Is this thank you enough, three great kids all living, a great wife and a bit of a limp, happy days !!!

She stops reading. The music stops. The BAND congratulate one another.

VIC *(Cont'd.)*
That's it!
(BEAT.)
Now you've left us thinking that the most important day in your life was when Blackpool got into the Premier League!

MIKE
Well there's a picture of me crying when we went up – I didn't cry when my kids were born.

VIC
Why would you even admit that? Don't you realise how that makes you look?

MIKE
I'm just saying...how many days do you get to experience pure joy?

VIC
(To audience.)
And he's been married to mum for 48 years and she only gets one sentence in this.

MIKE
Well we don't get on. We disagree on everything – I hate Emmerdale she hates news – I hate vacuum cleaners, she loves em.

Look Vic, your mum and I agreed at the beginning we'd do our own thing and not be a couple of park benchers – those couples you see sitting with nothing to say to each other...you see em in restaurants not talking to each other – it's so sad. We get around it by arguing all the time.

VIC
(Referring to his funeral plans.)
None of this is going to work dad. Do you know what'll happen if we bury you in the garden? It'll reduce the value of

the house by 50%. How are we going to get the barrel out of the hearse? Roll you out? And how we are going to fit you in the barrel, in the first place, chop your head off? And what about in 20 years time when we want to come and visit? We're going to knock on some poor sod's door – hi! Can we come and visit dad – he's buried under the rhododendrons. It's ridiculous! You haven't taken any of this seriously.

MIKE
At least my funeral's fun – it's not depressing and copied off the CO-OP. Yours was absolute poo. At least mine's a laugh and honest.

VIC
It's not honest though is it. It's just you taking the piss and farting around.

MIKE
Yeah but it's MY funeral. That's who I am.

> VIC sighs. She turns away and walks toward the audience, blocking MIKE, leaving him at the back of the stage stuck in his barrel.

VIC
(Like a TV presenter.)
I think what we've discovered here is that a funeral has to be somewhat for the people left behind. This is just dad saying stuff he wants to hear. Surely a eulogy should give meaning to someone's life – not just extend their chaos.
Can we change these lights please...?
> *(To BAND.)*
And can you play something...
factual?

> The BAND look at each other and start playing a corporate video underscore. VIC nods in approval.

LIGHTS CHANGE ... *(GOODBYE TANGERINE.)* /

BAND PLAYS CORPORATE VIDEO UNDERSCORE ...

MIKE
Hang on...what's going on?

VIC
(Continuing, to audience.)
However Dad has made some very good points – even if they wouldn't quite work in the real world – because there are actually LOADS of alternatives to the generic CO-OP funeral.

MIKE
What – did we finish that last bit then?

VIC
(Ignoring .)
You don't actually need a coffin – legally you can have a shroud...

MIKE
We were having a conversation. Why are you talking to them now?

VIC
And you don't even have to use a hearse, you can go in the back of a van if you want. It's even legal to be buried in your garden as long as you're not near a water source.

MIKE
(Firm now.)
Hang on – STOP!
    (BAND stop.)
Give me a light like hers please.

> *MIKE gets out of the barrel through a little door. VIC has to help him, he is ungainly getting out. VIC seems to be getting some joy out of pushing his head down to squeeze him out through the barrels little door. The BAND take the barrel away. MIKE is also wearing very unflattering orange Blackpool top.*

MIKE *(Cont'd.)*
    (To audience.)
I want to say something about this show. Vic said this would be a collaboration and it isn't! I've been working on this show for months – I'm well up for it don't get me wrong – but she's cut some of the best stuff out of it.

VIC
Like what?

MIKE
New Orleans.
(To audience.)
We actually went to New Orleans for this. You wouldn't know from this.
(To VIC.)
Why did you cut it? It was great!

VIC
It didn't fit the narrative arc.

MIKE
You keep saying that. Nobody understands what you're on about.
(Pointing at somebody in the audience.)
Apart from that bloke in the cravat.

VIC
It just didn't give us what we needed.

MIKE
...what YOU needed more like...

VIC
Well that's how theatre works – each bit has to earn its place in the story.

MIKE
Listen – you came to me and you said "Dad, let's collaborate on a show and make it a living funeral" I said great. But you're controlling all of it.

VIC turns to audience.
(Lighter change of mood.)

VIC
So that was acting. That was a reenactment of a real argument we had whilst devising the show.

MIKE
And guess who won.

> *VIC walks back and collects two antique chairs and sets them facing the curtains.*

VIC
So...we did go to New Orleans.

> *BAND start playing New Orleans music underscore.*

We went because dad said he wanted a jazz funeral...but also I thought it would be good research. We'd see how another culture deals with death. What connects and divides us?

Cause that's the show I wanted to make.

But it didn't really work out that way, did it Dad?

MIKE
(Crossing to sit in his chair.)
What do you mean? It was great.

> *VIC opens the curtains to reveal the screen.*

VIC
It wasn't. It was a disaster. Anyway, this is the New Orleans scene...that doesn't really fit the show.

> *She sits on chair next to MIKE.*

> *LIGHTS CHANGE.*

SCENE 8
NEW ORLEANS

BAND PLAYS Louder PERCUSSIVE IKO IKO piece under the following. VIC and MIKE are always facing towards the audience, legs swung round to the audience. They just move their heads to watch the screen.

VIC
(To audience.)
Dad's always said he's got this deep connection to New Orleans.
　　(To MIKE.)
Explain it to them.

MIKE

... I can't explain it, but somehow, I have a deep spiritual connection to the place. It's in me!

For some reason from age 12 – I loved soul and blues – Ray Charles "What i Say"/ Fats Domino, "Blueberry Hill". I realised all the music I like comes from New Orleans. I was walking over Runcorn Bridge homeless singing "Walking to New Orleans to go and sleep in a public toilet." –

Anyway FAST FORWARD 15 YEARS ... I went to New Orleans – to trade to the antique dealers on Royal Street.

They were the king and queen of Mardi Gras, they had a ball and me and Marg were the only British people invited other than the chairman and his wife of Wimbledon. How things change...

But it's a true story, we didn't know what to wear and I turned up in the full white tuxedo and everyone else wore dinner suits. People kept asking me for drinks all night they thought I was a waiter. I had it made by a tailer that suit, it costs hundreds. Never had a use for it since.

VIC

(VIC brings MIKE back from his story that's gone off tangent.)
OK. and... New Orleans and what it's got to do with the show?

MIKE

Oh and also – I've always loved their funerals – they're so great, they celebrate death...nothing like the repressed thing we do here. I thought it'd be perfect for the show.

VIC

So I agreed we should go.

> ON SCREEN: VT MIKE & VIC IN NEW ORLEANS – sights and
> sounds of the place. MIKE and VIC walking around the French
> quarter, looking at the stone crypts in St. Louis Cemetery
> No.1, eating a muffuletta sandwich in an old style bakery,
> being part of the congregation of a jazz second line funeral,
> watching a brass band on a street corner and sitting in bars
> watching bands. The music is infectious PRESERVATION HALL
> TYPE JAZZ MUSIC – that the band picks up and takes over.

MIKE
I was really revved! fried oysters, the gumbo, the music on Frenchman street...

VIC
(*Enthusiastic now.*)
And I put together this really good itinerary...

Dad rolls his eyes.

ON SCREEN: VIC'S RIDICULOUSLY DETAILED ITINERARY.

VIC *(Cont'd.)*
I lined up meetings with these key figures in the New Orleans funeral scene... I even scheduled in some relaxation time...

MIKE
To be honest I thought it was a load of poo but I've got to keep me mouth shut because it's a free trip.

VIC
So we got over there and I was really chuffed because I'd managed to persuade Cherice Nelson – who is the Big Queen of the Mardi Gras Indians – to do an interview. And when I told dad we were actually going to meet her, the first thing he said was:

MUSIC stops dead.

MIKE
"What's a Mardi Gras Indian?"

VIC
And it turns out, his entire knowledge of his beloved New Orleans jazz funeral comes from the first five minutes of LIVE AND LET DIE.

MIKE
Great scene.

ON SCREEN: CHERICE – meeting MIKE & VIC – they sit down...

VIC
This is Cherice, the Big Queen of the Guardians of the Flame Mardi Gras Indians...and we met her to talk about New Orleans funerals. The problem is dad kept interrupting all the time!

ON SCREEN: SEE SOME CLIPS OF DAD INTERRUPTING ...

Film clip of CHERICE, MIKE and VIC sitting in a conference room.

MIKE
In fact I've got to pick a religion to join yet. Because I'd bloody hate to be a pope and wonder up there and find some bloke in a yellow coat. "here you go son, shovel, you've picked the wrong mob." Laughs.

VIC and CHERICE don't find it funny. They don't know how to react so they carry on with what they were saying.

VIC
I'm taking dad to the Treme brass band tonight.

CHERICE
At the Candle Light Lounge?

VIC
Do we need to get there at 9pm or?

MIKE gets up from where we are seated and walks out of shot.

Back live in the theatre.

VIC *(Cont'd.)*
(To audience.)
...and this is Markeith Tero who is a funeral director and also the Grand Marshall at jazz funeral parades. And this is our interview...

ON SCREEN: INTERVIEW CLIPS OF MIKE INTERRUPTING / VIC GETTING ANNOYED. Markeith, MIKE and VIC sitting around a table outside in New Orleans.

VIC *(Cont'd.)*
The party, the big party in the street is a celebration of life and so what is it about your culture that makes you celebrate the deceased...

MIKE
(Interrupting.)
It's the only thing they've got!

61

VIC
No I want Markeith to answer!

MIKE and VIC argue. Markeith looks embarrassed.

VIC *(Cont'd.)*
So do you think it's the music that unites everybody...

MIKE
(Frustrated.)
I'm one thousand per cent certain...

MARKEITH
(Getting a word in.)
Once that bass drum strikes up or that trumpet or that tuba starts

Now MIKE is really frustrated with VIC's questions. He is answering all Markeith's questions for him even though MIKE is not a funeral director from New Orleans.

MIKE
Correct!

You've got to look at the background it might not be the same in a hundred years time because everybody will be driving a big Cadillac , duh, der duh.

VIC and Markeith have given up now and they are just letting MIKE talk at them. They don't know what he's going on about.

MIKE *(Cont'd.)*
In my case. It is really important that the psyche or even the tambourine.

VIC
(To MARKEITH.)
So it's the music?

MARKEITH
Yes it draws the attention

MIKE
(Interrupting.)
Game on

VIC
(MIKE has interrupted VIC she forgets what to say.)
Oh I've forgotten what to say now.

> *Awkward pause with nobody speaking.*

> *Back live in the theatre.*

VIC *(Cont'd.)*
And after a while it got me down. Plus dad kept wondering off during everything I'd arranged.

> *New clip of them on a guided tour in a cemetery MIKE walks off mid tour to go and sit on the bus.*

VIC *(Cont'd.)*
...but it quickly became obvious that all dad wanted to do was get pissed and listen to music in bars.

> *Clip of MIKE pissed and listening to music in a bar.*

Back live in the theatre
> *(To MIKE.)*
I mean where were you even walking off to?

MIKE
(To audience.)
It were boring. I can't see what the problem is. We went to New Orleans to bond.

VIC
No we went to WORK!
(To audience.)
And he didn't do any.

MIKE
She didn't let her hair down. I had an amazing time. And I'll tell you when I walked down Royal Street – I was a king!

VIC
Dad, who would admit to that? You just used you and "king" in the same sentence.

MIKE
Legend then.

(*To audience.*)
Our Vic's always been pissed off with me. I don't mind. Do you know the bit that wound her up the most?

VIC
...it didn't wind me up...

MIKE
She won't admit this...but when we met that Big Queen woman – she'd been talking about her dad who died – now this man had been Big Chief of the Guardians of the Galaxy or whatever...

VIC
Guardians of the Flame Mardi Gras Indians!

MIKE
Correct! Anyway, halfway through, she has this moment when I'm talking – and she looks straight at me...here, I'll show you...

ON SCREEN: VT CHERICE. *They are still sitting in the conference room.*

CHERICE
Even when you are walking out

MIKE
(*Interrupting.*)
That's in a song that.

CHERICE
What?

MIKE
Nobody gets out alive

CHERICE
Yeah my daddy used to tell me that but I didn't know it was in a song.

MIKE
It's in a song
(*Trying to think.*)
Shit, I think it's one of the best lines of all time. I'm pretty sure it was Ray Charles.

CHERICE
Well my daddy loved Ray Charles.

MIKE
It's called three Quarter time it's a waltz , right...

CHERICE
(Interrupting.)
Oh my God my daddy's in this room, he's in you. I'm serious.
My daddy is in your body and talking to me. I am so serious.

MIKE
Great, fine.
(Pause.)
Thank you.

    Back live in the theatre.

MIKE (Cont'd.)
She thought I was carrying the spirit of the Big Chief himself...
    (To VIC.)
You wanted to know why New Orleans was my spiritual home?
There's the proof!! A king I tell you! And Vic didn't like it.

VIC
(To audience, she's deflated.)
I wasn't wound up by it. I was just relieved he didn't take the
piss.

I liked it that her dad went inside my dad. We were trying to find
out why New Orleans was dad's spiritual home – now Big Chief
was going inside Ugly Chief! That wasn't what annoyed me.
    (Shared not performed.)
To tell the truth I found the whole trip stressful. For me, the
reason we went there was to find out about other people and
all he wanted to do was talk about himself. Cherice was telling
us about how nobody ever cries at Mardi Gras Indian funerals.
If you feel sad then drummers come and make a circle around
you. She said that "nobody ever cries in the circle" THAT IS
BEAUTIFUL! But dad interrupted her to tell a story, nothing to
do with drummers about when he went fishing in Grand Isle
and they used crayfish for bait and he would rather eat the
bait than the fish. That's why I was pissed off!

MIKE
(Dismissive.)
She was jet lagged. She does suffer from quite severe jetlag.

VIC
(Biting her tongue.)
I wasn't jet lagged. I was holding it all together. I kept a video diary while I was there. This is me on day five.

> *ON SCREEN: VIC's video diary confessional. VIC talks direct to camera. She is alone in a hotel room. She looks sad, pensive and almost on the verge of tears.*

I'm in a mood. I'm in a massive mood that I need to snap out of. I'm probably a bit more uptight because I'm thinking about the bigger picture. The bigger picture of the show and the bigger picture about what we are doing here.

Maybe I am a bit uptight but everyone we meet really loves dad and they say "make sure he makes friends with us on facebook" and all this kind of thing. Where as they...you know
> *(PAUSE.)*
they are less keen about staying in touch with me.

The main problem is I can't control him. I think that's it. He's uncontrollable, he's doing his own thing and he's not respecting that I need some level of control. He doesn't really deal with hangovers very well. His actual body if he's hungover or in drink...he really can't control his leg. He can't get his leg in a car, he has to physically lift his leg like it's a piece of dead meat and put it in the car. And I don't really like seeing him like that.

> *When we come back from this clip, instead of appealing to the audience for support, VIC & MIKE talk to each other.*

VIC *(Cont'd.)*
(Said quietly down to her lap.)
That's why I didn't want the New Orleans section in – because it's not about funerals, it's about us.

MIKE
What's wrong with that?

VIC
Dad, I wanted to do a comedy show that would be part living funeral for you...but also a show that looked at traditions and our attitudes to death. I didn't want to deconstruct our relationship.

MIKE
It's the same thing.

VIC
How?

MIKE
If you want to know how much an antique's worth, you've got to know the history – everything that made it – we call it provenance. It's the same here. If you want to give me a living funeral – you've got to look at the whole picture. Good and bad. Can't just whitewash everything.

VIC
But I'm talking about how difficult you are.

MIKE
No, you're talking about how you feel.

MIKE walks up to address the audience.

MIKE *(Cont'd.)*
Vic's problem is she hides her feelings behind rituals and traditions and facts..."Here's the eulogy I was TRAINED to give" / "I've got a PROPER questionnaire that FUNERAL DIRECTORS USE" / I've researched this/I've field worked that/ narrative arc the other... She's a robot.

VIC walks downstage to defend herself.

VIC
(To audience.)
That's really unfair. This show's making me sound really uptight. And I can tit tassel.

I don't see what this has to do with me – a funeral is meant to praise the person who's gone.

MIKE
Who says it should praise them?

VIC
It's in the CO-OP brochure: How to Write a Eulogy.

MIKE
You just proved my point!!
Look – blow tradition, bollocks to training, throw that bloody brochure away and connect with your feelings. Hey! Look at me.
    (VIC turns to him.)
You came to me and said lets collaborate on a show. 50/50.
    (VIC nods.)
We did the first half that you wanted. I hated it but I went along with it. So now it's my turn, let me have the second half. That's fair, yes?

    VIC shrugs.

MIKE *(Cont'd.)*
Yes?

VIC
YES!

MIKE
(To audience.)
So that was acting. That was a reenactment of an argument we had during rehearsal.

VIC
(Resigned.)
And guess who won.

MIKE
So welcome to the Mike Melody show.

    LIGHTS UP.

SCENE 9
THE MIKE MELODY SHOW

BAND gets two TV interviews show chairs. BAND play "MIKE's Excitement Theme". MIKE is all showbiz energy and has a prosecutor's drive throughout the following scene. Music continues to underscore.

MIKE
Now first of all, I'd like to go back to your eulogy for me that you read in the first half. Which I thought was safe...

> *VIC gets two eulogies from the lectern she passes one to MIKE. Through this next section the BAND quietly try to underscore but they can't get the emotional quality right. They are trying but they are perplexed and not sure what is appropriate. The underscoring therefore sounds messy and unpleasant, they are out of sync with one another. They are irritated.*

VIC
(Thrown away.)
Here you go, yours is the one with giant writing.
> *(To audience, she's exasperated.)*

He's so ungrateful. I lovingly crafted that eulogy so people would be interested by you so they would like you.

MIKE
It was charming...there's nothing charming about me. It was safe. Tell the real truth and you get the real person. Like this bit...
> *(To audience.)*

Do you remember the bit when she said *"I had an interesting upbringing"*?
That was a bit loaded wasn't it?
> *(To VIC.)*

What did you mean by that?

VIC
Well, it was just...weird, wasn't it.

MIKE
Say weird then. Why not say you had a weird upbringing?
> *(BEAT.)*

Go on then. What was weird about it?

VIC
All of it.

MIKE
Let's hear it then.

VIC
(To audience.)
So for this bit dad asked me to go off and do an exercise where I wrote down answers to his questions...

I really don't see the point of this...

MIKE
Just get on with it!

VIC
(Reading.)
Question: What did you mean when you said you had an "interesting upbringing?"

OK, well: When I was little, dad bought me a Wendy house – apart from it wasn't a Wendy house it was a shed where he kept his tools.

MIKE
It was an Edwardian Summer house.

VIC
No it wasn't... This is also where he kept my quad bike – only it wasn't a quad bike it was a second hand mobility scooter"

MIKE
Rare model / 60s design concept...

VIC
Also, he used to rescue dogs from the death row at the RSPCA and give them to me even though he was warned they shouldn't be around kids. But when the dogs died – down to old age or because they'd got run over on the busy road outside our house – he would bury them around my Wendy house – but never deep enough.

MIKE
You should have seen that quad bike go over the bumps at one MPH.

VIC
(To audience.)
That's what I mean by weird.

MIKE
Give us another example.

VIC
All right, what about the time you told me the facts of life when I was seven?
    (To audience.)
Do you know what he said? He said you're a woman, all men will try and sleep with you. You need to keep your legs crossed. I would have shagged a tea pot when I was a lad.

MIKE
What's wrong with that?

VIC
I was SEVEN! I only asked you if a period was a pill a lady took to get pregnant. That was my level of awareness.

MIKE
See if it were me, I'd put that in the eulogy. I think you need some examples to back up the point about the weird upbringing.

Also in Vic's eulogy she said: I "*wasn't always easy to live with*". Please read your answer...

VIC
Dad was really unhygienic. He farted constantly and he'd sit on the toilet for an hour reading his newspaper cover to cover with the door open stinking out the house with poo.

And he never cleaned his teeth. He spent 10 grand getting his teeth done. Then didn't bother to clean them so they fell out again.

And what about the time two years ago at Xmas when we were playing Chinese whispers as a family and he started the whole whisper off by saying into my ear– "Vic is barren."

MIKE
Come on, that is funny.

VIC
Yes but it's wrong on so many levels. What if I couldn't have kids?

MIKE
Well you haven't.

VIC
Cause I've CHOSEN not to. It's a CHOICE!

MIKE
(Next question.)
Anyway Vic, in your bland eulogy you said...
    (Quoting.)
"I packed my suitcase at 16 never to return". And then: As the saying goes blood is thicker than water."

What the bloody hell does that mean?

VIC
I didn't know what else to say about leaving home.

MIKE
Which leads us nicely to the next question I asked Vic to write down:

Why did you leave home?

VIC
(Killing the conversation dead.)
No!

MIKE
Why won't you answer?

VIC
I don't want people to hate you.

(To audience.)
Most dads would get upset to have their daughter criticize them in public. But he wants it. It just bounces off him like water off a duck's back. I think he actually likes it.
(Getting off the stool and leaving sheet of paper on the stool.)
Sorry dad but this isn't the show I wanted to make. People don't want to see us air our dirty laundry.

MIKE
Yeah they do...
(To audience.)
Don't you?

Audience cheer.

See?

VIC
That was two people and I think they only cheered because they felt guilty.

MIKE
(With force.)
Not fair Vic! I did everything you wanted in Part One –
I answered all your questions in that questionnaire scene that went on forever at the end. Why can't you do this?

Reluctantly, eventually, VIC gets her sheet of paper and sits back on stool.

VIC
Reasons why I left home at 16:
Number One – I couldn't rely on him for anything. He used to forget to pick me up from primary school so the Lollipop Lady would take me home with her. And then the Lollipop Lady got the sack because she wasn't allowed to take children home.

MIKE
I'd forgotten about that...

VIC
What a surprise.
Two – There was that time when we were in Marbella when I ran up to the seafood restaurant where he & mum were

boozing and I fell and split my head open on the steps and you stayed in the restaurant drinking and eating whilst a total stranger put me on his shoulders and ran with mum and me to an infirmary to get stitches. Why didn't you take me to the infirmary?

MIKE
I couldn't speak Spanish and the fish was amazing...

The BAND sense that they need to stop playing.

VIC
Three: You TOTALLY DOMINATED MUM!!
She worked in that shop six days a week all year round bringing in the money while you pissed it away playing Football Manager on the computer and making shit business decisions.

Four: You were violent when you were drunk. Do you know that Mum and I genuinely spent an evening looking at the criteria of psychopath and sociopath to decide which one you are.

Five: You never listened to anyone – and if you DID seem like you were listening, it's only because you were thinking about what you were going to say next.

And by the way, the only reason I liked being in that music room was because it was the only time I ever got any attention – but then I got older and I realised you were just drunk and it was just another chance for you to talk AT someone and none of it mattered because NOTHING affects you and NOTHING hurts you.
    (BEAT.)
Do you really want that in your eulogy?

A LONG SILENCE.

After eight seconds, he goes to say something. VIC looks at him expectantly. Another long silence passes.

MIKE
Look, Vic... I know I need to say something here... I just...
    (He trails off.)

I never know how to say these things.
Can I play you a song?
    (To the BAND.)
Can you play Cry to Me?

> *The BAND come out from their seats and stand centre stage in front of the curtains. They never return to play in that old configuration again. They are now part of the chaos. They play CRY TO ME by Solomon Burke. A verse passes with MIKE just looking at VIC, hoping she'll get it. Then he starts mouthing along, getting more into it. By the second chorus he is lip syncing perfectly, dancing round the music room. MIKE need to only face VIC and the audience when he sings. It ends. He goes back to his stool.*

VIC
That's it?
(To audience.)
He always used to do this. Play a song instead of speaking to us.
    (Hopeful pause but nothing.)
Oh, why don't you just carry on with your half?

MIKE
(Relieved.)
Great!

VIC
(Looking around.)
This stage is a shithole.

> *VIC move's about the stage tidying up the debris from MIKE's funeral. The BAND start clearing up their music equipment (quietly!) They are subtly placing their instruments around stage for the next bits.*

> *MIKE comes forward to front of stage centre to deliver the following text.*

MIKE
Well I'd like to do a scene about Vic's first dog. Vic and I really bonded over that dog.

VIC
(Cutting him off.)
And then dad killed the dog.

MIKE
Hang on I'll have the RSPCA after me. I ran him over. It was an accident. Aright that was a bad example let's do a story about you at art college...

VIC
Why, what's that got do with anything?

MIKE
(Ignores VIC and speaks to audience.)
Obviously Vic and I had severe differences in which resulted in her leaving home. But I think when Vic and I really became friends was when she was doing art at Northumbria Uni. She thrived there – it was like watching a flower grow – we were on the phone every week...weren't we Vic?

VIC
(Resigned.)
It's true – I found myself calling him up and just talking. Something between us had shifted. It turned out that compared to the rest of the family, dad and I were quite similar – we had an anarchic sense of humour – although his politics are disgusting.

It got so that – these days my sisters say if dad dies, everyone wants mum to live with them. If mum goes then they say dad has to live with me.

MIKE
I'd changed my tack by then. I'd got my drinking under control – I had regrets about how I'd been with Vic when she was younger and so I wasn't imposing my will on her – I let her run things.

Anyway, she had a visiting lecturer at her college who really loved her work and he said he'd help her apply for a scholarship to do a Masters at Chelsea College of Art. I didn't think she had half a prayer. I was made up when she got in. I was proud of her.

(To VIC.)
But tell em what it was like when you got there, Vic.

VIC has been sweeping up the sawdust that is meant to signify MIKE's BBQ pit. She stops tidying the stage for a moment and talks to the audience.

VIC
I was really looking forward to it. I was awarded a prestigious bursary. It was my first time living in London... But I hated it. It was unfriendly. It was a dog eat dog atmosphere.

I would be in the front of the queue for the editing suite and people would push in front of me saying "my needs are greater than yours".

Students leaned their paintings up against a wall for an art competition, And somebody came in over night and slashed the best paintings.

I felt intimidated. In one lecture, the lecturer turned to me and asked me a question about Baudrillard and simulacra, I didn't know what to say and it felt like I'd wee'ed myself. Only I hadn't.

MIKE
She used to ring me up especially when times were grim to ask my advice.

She'd be telling me about Chelsea on the phone – she was working like a dog, trying her best – on one call she sounded so down. So I said – look you've got two choices: nobody'll think bad of you if you come home – but if you feel so angry, why don't you do something that shows them you're angry. Tell them to "fuck off!!".

VIC
I'm not quite as blunt as dad to be able to tell people to fuck off. But I knew he was right. I thought about this. So I made a video and left invites to the screening on everyone's table who'd been a bastard.

So now, here, as requested by dad, is a video of our first ever art collaboration.

By now the stage is completely clear of debris apart from two chairs facing the screen with backs to the audience. The BAND are standing looking at the audience in two's both sides of the screen. GEMMA's keyboard is set up

ON SCREEN: PISSED-OFF PUMPKIN VT. This is a film VIC made in 2001. She has dark hair and a young face and a much plumper appearance. She is alone in a white room wearing a large inflatable pumpkin costume. She has an old fashioned megaphone. She is looking into the camera whilst dancing and saying Fuck Off but she is more lackadaisical than aggressive. It is very funny.

MUSIC: BAND.) PLAY "Fuck off"...quietly at first under the tail end of the video, but building under the following speech, it's a minimalist Philip Glass style song.

VIC *(Cont'd.)*
And the strange thing is that everyone at Chelsea thought it was BRILLIANT! They read all sort of hidden meanings into it. In the feedback they kept asking me – *"who is your intended audience for this piece?"* And I said: You. They saw the megaphone as a metaphor and they were asking me *"what did you intend by the megaphone?"* I said – I intended to tell you to fuck off. They thought that was brilliant too. I got a distinction, won an award, got a residency at a gallery... Encouraged, I followed Pissed-Off Pumpkin up with Bastard Bee and Bemused Bear – I had a whole franchise going – Marvel had nothing on me.

MIKE is in his chair, watching all this. He applauds.

MIKE
That was great! I really enjoyed that. Much better than the first half. The second half became a very surprising and moving portrait of how a father initially sabotages but ultimately helps his daughter.
Right, I'm off now.
(To BAND.)

Come on you lot...

> One of the BAND closes the curtains. The BAND pick up
> their instruments and start, playing a light arrangement of A
> CLOSER WALK WITH THEE. They take MIKE and VIC's chairs
> with them. Leaving the stage completely clear.

VIC
(To Mike.)
Where are you going?

MIKE
We've put everything in I wanted. I'm happy.

VIC
You said you wanted to have the second half. It's not over.

MIKE
It is for me.

> He starts walking off, the BAND following.

VIC
(To BAND.)
And where are you going?

BAND
It is his half, Vic...you did say.

VIC
That's not a half! My half was funny – it had devices and
musical cues and we learned things about traditions and
Britishness. Your half was chaos!

MIKE
My half had pathos. It's the half that bloke in the cravat will
give all the stars to.

VIC
You said we were collaborating!

MIKE
It was always your show Vic. I'm not a thespian.
    (Getting to the door.)
You've got all the material you need. Now go and give me a eulogy.

LIGHTS!!!

LIGHTS UP – IT IS NOW BLINDING WHITE LIGHT ON STAGE – everything stripped away.

MIKE leaves with the BAND in tow – the strains of CLOSER WALK can be heard fading out in the lobby. VIC is furious but we wouldn't know it as VIC is offstage yelling into the foyer at MIKE.)

SCENE 10
VIC'S FINAL EULOGY

VIC
How is this my show?!! You took it over and now you're pissing off. My show would have been full of the amazing characters I met and...dad... DAD?

But he is gone. VIC is hopping mad, virtually spitting the words out. Lots of energy, frustrated. FUCKING FED UP. This is delivered as stream of consciousness. VIC has been restrained through the whole show and this is her release. This is MIKE's gift to her.

VIC (Cont'd.)
(To audience.)
MY show would have been better than this. We would have found out how every one of those people who work in that funeral home lead these incredible double lives! One is in a brilliant Welsh choir and they sing to royalty, another is a famous world champion chicken fancier – Howard – who works at the crematorium – races against horses. Not ON horses – AGAINST horses. We would have learned that they don't do this for escapism – it's people EMBRACING INTENSE EXPERIENCES OF LIFE because they're in touch with their mortality. We would have seen how they're a COMMUNITY and they SUPPORT each other, how they treat each other with RESPECT – how it was the first time I ever felt like I belonged to a family! Did you know that Gareth actually offered me a job? I always thought I was unemployable.

There's a video clip of it but I didn't get to show it. But he said
"If the art goes tits up, there's always a position for you here.
You are a natural and we all enjoyed your presence.
You are now an honorary Welsh girl – Victoria Blodwyn
Melody. Blodwyn! BLODWYN!

But we're not doing any of that because we're doing this.

She is pacing the stage, fizzing off in all directions...

All right... I'll give you a eulogy...

Dearly Beloved, we are gathered here today to celebrate
the life of Michael Anthony Dominic Fucking Melody. What a
juvenile, selfish, tosser he was. Do you know sometimes I think
my life would have been better if my dad was Keith Harris.
      (Finding the words as she goes.)
Mike Melody created chaos in his wake wherever he went and
he left it up to everybody else to pick up the pieces...
      (Improvising.)
He knew the value of things but not of people.
      (Here's another one.)
His parenting skills were using one of his own words SHITE.
The reason I left home at 16 was because I fucking hated him.

All right then... I'll tell you one moment that summed up
our relationship: The time he picked me up from the hotel
on my wedding day to take me to get married. I had high
hopes for what this drive would be like...with just the two of
us. I imagined he'd act like a normal dad – he'd say I looked
beautiful, say he was proud, maybe pass on some wisdom,
share something tender.

He pulled up outside the hotel. The car seat had pie crumbs all
over it. I tried to brush them off, to stop them soiling my dress.
He said stop mithering and get in. Then with the windows up,
he lit a fag, the smoke went in my eyes.

VIC *(Cont'd.)*
And it was a Saturday so he was listening to the football on
the radio. The whole journey was a total let down.
      (LONG PAUSE, remembering.)
On the way, we stopped so I could wee. In a pub not in a lay-by.

(Thrown away.)
Although I have done that.

When I got back in the car. Dad was having a fag outside so I waited. Then through the closed window – I saw him looking at me and he mouthed the words "I love you".

Then he got back in and we drove the rest of the journey in silence.

> *A long six seconds pause. When she speaks her tone has changed, she is reflective.*

VIC *(Cont'd.)*
That was us all over.
> *(Another LONG BEAT.)*
I always used to joke that when I looked at dad it was like looking at everything I dislike about me.
But I never fully understood how true that was until I started working on this show.
(BEAT.)
I'm the same as him.
> *(BEAT.)*
EVERYTHING we do is convoluted.
What kind of daughter would deal with her feelings for her dad by roping him into a dress rehearsal for his funeral, and hire musicians, costumes and a customized barrel on wheels? And what kind of father would agree to this and then push her to say the worst things she could about him and lay himself open to the judgement of strangers?
> *(Pointing around the stage.)*
This isn't a normal way for people to say they love each other.
BUT ALL THIS IS SAFE.

It's only when we're about to really lose someone or after they've actually gone that we know what to say...or should have said.

If I could have been honest, I would have said the reason I was angry with him in New Orleans wasn't because he wanted to get pissed in bars. I was angry with him because that trip made me realise he's frail and he's getting old and I don't want him to die.

And if I'd been really honest, instead of putting so much thought into finding the right words for after he's gone, I'd have been honest and said what I really want to say:

I'm not ready to let him go.

She steps back. The stage is white. MIKE has been watching this from the side. VIC walks out.

MIKE walks centre stage. He is wearing a white tuxedo complete with frilly shirt and bow tie. He put's his reading glasses on and takes a crumpled piece of paper out of his pocket and begins to read.

SCENE 11
MIKE'S EULOGY FOR VIC

MIKE
If I was ever to be in the sad position of writing an eulogy about Vic it would go something like this Our Vic was born on Friday 13th January sometime in the 80s.
She was second of what turned out to be three kids. It was an unremarkable birth only remembered for a large red birth mark on her face, an omen maybe.
Aged 2 she fell down a flight of stone stairs banging her head which hospitalised her and may explain certain strange traits she developed.

Still as a little fighter she soon left hospital and continued to live her life.

Maybe this is where her fighting spirit came from. Village school was a Welsh primary and it was only when we discovered she couldn't tell the time at the age of 9 we took an interest in her education. Her elder sister Georgie was so perfect. We assumed things. I'm afraid that period sums up my parenthood... SHITE.

Around the age of 14 things got serious. We discovered she was being bullied at the school we sent George too. At this time I really felt for her as she cut a lonely figure walking three miles home rather than catch the school bus. Art and Music came into her life, it was a joy to see but with it came the teenage years. Life at home became impossible. I threw her out of the house when she was 16.

I think my first real love of Vic as a daughter was when she didn't come back. I was secretly proud, silly ain't it. When we eventually, to use a well hackneyed phrase...bonded, it was like meeting a new person.

The Vic you all know and possibly love is the one I met after her own personal traumas, which I'm sure were plenty, is the confident, caring, intelligent person she grew into.

Everything our Vic said about me in the show is true. I was a despot. I'm not proud of it. Looking back I give myself one out of ten for parenting. It took a long while for me to see that.

But my daughter Vic by the side of me is a shining example of what proper love can achieve.

Now as I contemplate dotage, she who through her own efforts and tribulations, came through the carnage to become one of the nicest warmest most pleasant people I have ever met.

> PAUSE – three drum beats. MIKE walks stage right and waits. A New Orleans funeral dirge can be heard from outside the room as VIC re-enters, dressed in her inflatable Pumpkin Suit, followed by THE BAND.

> VIC and MIKE face each other as the BAND surround them.

> The BAND create a drumming circle around VIC and MIKE which references CHERICE Nelson's New Orleans drumming circles. Where "nobody ever cries in the circle". The BAND come out into a semi circle. VIC and MIKE bow to each other. Now they circle each other in a sombre, deliberate dance, coming together MIKE's left arm is facing the audience. MIKE and VIC have trouble getting his arm up on her shoulder, it's awkward but funny. They come together in a broken waltz.

NOW THE MUSICIANS, VIC AND MIKE CUT LOOSE – a FAST, INFECTIOUS SOUND.

VIC and MIKE both bow their heads. All take their bows and exit still playing music, they all leave in a New Orleans style procession.

END.

An Interview with Mike

What does it feel like to be misdiagnosed with a terminal illness?

I was originally told I had the advent of motor neurone disease, which I hadn't a clue what it was. We had to Google it to find out. When the whole thing unravelled and it turned out I hadn't got it was like winning the lottery all I can say is "happy days".

What has it been like working on *Ugly Chief*?

If I'd known what I was getting into I probably would be still hopping away. Maybe hiding in the Gobi desert. It has introduced me to a whole new world I never knew existed. The efforts of all are immense. Unfortunately I'm the weak link. A thespian I will never make.

What's it been like working with your daughter?

Working with Vic as the boss has been incredibly stressful for her and a walk in the park for me. We both know how to wind each other up so we have had to develop a neutral zone, which we are still working on but we are both secure enough to appreciate one another's love.

Have you enjoyed working on the show?

Enjoyment would be too weak a word. I've absolutely loved the build up to this show. The stand out moments include freezing me butt off in the Spire Church in Brighton whilst pontificating from a marble pulpit (don't ask!) Staying in an Easy Hotel in Edinburgh big enough for an active hamster whilst performing the part show in an ex animal hospital, the name escapes me.*

New Orleans was I'm sure a trip designed to keep me on board and it did! Ipswich** was another highlight of my fledgling thespian career. My van got broken into on the night the Mighty Pool beat Luton.

Sharing houses with vegan nut eaters, gluten free of course kept my menu anticipation at an all time low. It really has been a roller coaster I'm still recovering from. All of which have provided me with one of my best experiences in recent times.

*Summerhall

** Pulse Festival at the New Wolsey

WWW.OBERONBOOKS.COM

Follow us on www.twitter.com/@oberonbooks
& www.facebook.com/OberonBooksLondon

www.ingramcontent.com/pod-product-compliance
Ingram Content Group UK Ltd.
Pitfield, Milton Keynes, MK11 3LW, UK
UKHW020724280225
455688UK00012B/500

9 781786 823700